UNTO US A CHILD IS BORN

A CHRISTMAS DEVOTIONAL

25 Reflections of Promises Fulfilled

by
Emory Colvin Hornaday

Copyright © 2024 by Emory Colvin Hornaday
All rights reserved.

No portion of this book may be reproduced in any form without written permission from the publisher or author, except as permitted by U.S. copyright law.

Unless otherwise indicated, all Scripture quotations are taken from THE HOLY BIBLE, NEW INTERNATIONAL VERSION®, NIV® Copyright © 1973, 1978, 1984, 2011 by Biblica, Inc.® Used by permission. All rights reserved worldwide.

Scripture quotations marked NLT are taken from the Holy Bible, New Living Translation, copyright © 1996, 2004, 2015 by Tyndale House Foundation. Used by permission of Tyndale House Publishers, Inc., Carol Stream, Illinois 60188. All rights reserved.

Scripture quotations marked CSB have been taken from the Christian Standard Bible®, Copyright © 2017 by Holman Bible Publishers. Used by permission. Christian Standard Bible® and CSB® are federally registered trademarks of Holman Bible Publishers.

For reproduction inquiries visit www.emorycolvin.com.

Cover Design By: Jandré Van Der Walt
Author Photo: Cayton Heath Photography

ENDORSEMENTS

Emory Hornaday is a special gift to the body of Christ, expertly crafting creative expressions that explore the depths of the divine. Her newest book, *Unto Us a Child is Born,* is full of fresh poetic perspective on the birth of our Savior that will take you on a journey through the Scriptures to see the astounding ability of God to keep His promises.

Kris Vallotton
Senior Associate Leader, Bethel Church, Redding, CA
Co-Founder of Bethel School of Supernatural Ministry
Author of fifteen books, including The Supernatural Ways of Royalty, Spiritual Intelligence, *and* Uprising

Language is both powerful and beautiful. Its Creator is the consummate Communicator. His words are living and active and sharper than any two-edged sword. His Son is the Word who became flesh and dwelt among us, the reason that we celebrate Christmas. Emory Hornaday has harnessed the power and beauty of language to present afresh the prophetic words that announced the birth of the Word, Jesus Christ. Through her God-given craft as a poet, Emory has rekindled the wonder of treasured Scriptures cloaked by familiarity. *Unto Us a Child is Born* integrates poetry and theology. How fitting! The Old Testament prophets were poets.

Unto Us a Child is Born will challenge readers to plumb the depth of twenty-five Old or New Testament prophecies and to apply those ancient words that never age. Using Emory's devotional, readers will be prepared to worship the Savior throughout the season of Advent.

Dr. Ivan Parke
Professor and Assistant to the Chair of Christian Studies, Mississippi College
Author of When Life Meets the Soul *and* Reclaiming the Real Jesus

Nothing has changed the world as much as the life of Jesus Christ. Whether you follow Him or not, it's clear that His time on Earth had, and continues to have, an eternal impact on humanity. This momentous occasion is certainly worthy of celebration, but it becomes even richer and more meaningful when we understand the hundreds of prophecies He fulfilled in His short time on Earth. Emory Hornaday has created a unique treasure trove of poetic explorations expressed through the creative linguistic gift God has given her, that is truly remarkable. Each poem offers a fresh and insightful perspective on the stories and prophecies of Jesus, shedding new light on both the familiar and the obscure. Each chapter includes a unique biblical prophecy and its fulfillment, reinforcing the hope that God faithfully completes what He begins.

As we celebrate His birth this season and every season, this book makes a wonderful addition to your yearly family traditions. Discover a fresh understanding of Jesus's work and significance as you explore this season with new eyes and a renewed heart.

Bethany Hicks
Co-founder of Prophetic Company
Author of Own Your Assignment, The God Connection,
and The Power in a Name

In *Unto Us a Child is Born*, author Emory Hornaday explores the hope and longing of God's people contained in selected biblical prophetic voices which are fulfilled, i.e., "filled full," in Jesus of Nazareth who is God's Messiah, the Christ. Emory's erudite poetry and engaging exercises will challenge and comfort the celebrant who seeks a deeper, richer experience during the festivals of Advent and Christmastide. "Joy to the world, the Lord is come."

Edward Mahaffey, Ph.D.
Professor of Christian Studies, Mississippi College

Unto Us a Child is Born weaves the prophetic with the promise creating a mosaic of celebration and joy. The power in this lyrical experience is the strong scriptural connection to each line and verse. Through a poetic lens, Hornaday guides readers on a 25-day journey, each day reflecting on a different prophecy and its fulfillment in Jesus. The book captures the anticipation and fulfillment of the Messiah's coming, emphasizing themes of hope, redemption, and divine promise. It challenged me to explore the depth of God's plan from Genesis to the Gospels. She invites us to experience the wonder of the Christmas story anew. Hornaday's creative adaptations encourage personal reflection and a deeper appreciation of the birth of Christ, making this devotional a meaningful addition to Advent and Christmas observances.

Unto Us a Child is Born has staying power. It will be a source of inspiration and a prompt to worship for many Christmases to come.

Matt Tullos
Author of Uh Oh, Aha *and* Glory Be!
Church Specialist, Tennessee Baptist Mission Board

It's an honor to endorse Emory Hornaday's forthcoming devotional. Emory is a brilliant poet whose words carry the weight of both beauty and truth. In this Advent-themed work, she masterfully weaves together prophetic insights with the rich tradition of Jesus' birth, offering readers a deep and poetic exploration of the reason for the season. Her gift for spoken word shines through in every page, inviting us to pause, reflect, and encounter the prophetic promises that lead to the manger.

Emory is not only a dear friend but also a prophetic voice for this hour, and her work is sure to bless and inspire all who read it.

Justin Allen
Author of Confessions of a Young Prophet
Founder, Times and Seasons Coaching/Consulting

Emory Hornaday's words offer a beautiful exploration and invitation into the larger story we belong to as believers, drawing the reader's heart deeply into the significance of Christ's birth. This book is rich in theology while remaining accessible, with guided prayers that awaken the heart to profoundly connect not only with the selected Scripture passages, but also with the Lord Himself. A wonderful and powerful work!

Jonna Schuster
Co-Founder and Director of Catholic Revival Ministries

DEDICATION

This book is dedicated to the great cloud of witnesses who pronounced the coming of Christ, who persevered in faith believing that salvation was coming, who were persecuted, some even unto death, holding on to the hope of the promised Messiah. He has come, and He has delivered us. As Hebrews 11 states, together, we will be made perfect. I honor those who have gone before, fulfilling their call, and I commit to fight my good fight until I am called home to join you.

In him was life, and that life was the light of all mankind. The light shines in the darkness, and the darkness has not overcome it.
John 1:4–5

TABLE OF CONTENTS

Foreword	11
Introduction	13
December 1	14
December 2	25
December 3	33
December 4	41
December 5	49
December 6	56
December 7	63
December 8	71
December 9	79
December 10	86
December 11	93
December 12	99
December 13	107
December 14	114
December 15	122
December 16	130
December 17	137
December 18	144
December 19	151
December 20	158
December 21	165
December 22	172
December 23	180
December 24	190
December 25	198
Conclusion	206
Acknowledgments	208

FOREWORD

The advent of the birth of Jesus, the Christ, is the most pivotal event in human history. Yet, the virgin birth of God's son is also deeply and profoundly personal. Twenty-eight hundred years before we were born, the prophet Isaiah made it personal when he penned, "Unto us a child is born. Unto us a son is given." The promise of the coming Messiah was not intended for an isolated audience of a particular religious sect; it was predetermined before the creation of the world for all who would believe.

As such, the Christmas celebration is much more than the commemoration of a Bible story, it is the joyful and personal recognition of the cumulative fulfillment of thousands of years of prophetic promise. The author, Emory Hornaday, has masterfully gathered those millennia of biblical predictions and woven them into something that is both practical and accessible to every one of us. Her poetic adaptations of Scripture take us on a journey through time to experience the longing of generations fulfilled in the person of Jesus Christ.

I challenge you to complete this pilgrimage through time and prophecy to experience the true joy of Christmas in the coming of God Himself in human form. Whether you travel alone in your personal exploration, make it a family devotion, or bring others along in a group study, may the weight of this glorious experience be fully encountered by all who dare take this path. Unwrap the wonderful, personal gift of the Advent of Jesus Christ and see this season in a way you perhaps never have before.

Dan McCollam
American author and trainer
Co-founder of Prophetic Company, The SQ Institute, and Bethel School of the Prophets

INTRODUCTION

I've always found the prophecies of the Bible to be fascinating. How does one know the future? How could so many different people, over the span of hundreds of years accurately predict future events? And yet, we have a text full of "the word of the Lord" from the mouths of Old Testament prophets and their divine fulfillment in the New Testament. As readers of both the Old and New Testaments, what do these prophecies and fulfillments hold for us? What can we learn from them? Do they have any applications for us today? With these questions in mind, I began my journey of reading and writing about the Advent of Jesus.

The idea for this book first came to me in 2019 when I was looking for a way to commemorate Advent, but couldn't find a resource that didn't seem to be geared toward families with young children and chocolate behind daily doors (not that I'm opposed to a daily dose of chocolate!). I am thrilled to now know that there are several such resources, but at that time my search came up short. I wanted to create a book that deepened the meaning behind the Christmas season and that was accessible to anyone, single or married, with children or without. The only requirement would be a hunger for divine connection, a desire to celebrate this sacred time leading up to the messy and miraculous birth of our Savior.

Though it took some time, you now hold the result of my longing in your hands. This is not your typical Christmas devotional book! Each day explores a prophecy made prior to the birth of Christ that found its fulfillment within His coming. My prayer is that this unique format draws you to think in a new way about something that may have become familiar over time.

I hope you enjoy my exploration of some of the prophecies surrounding Jesus' birth. While Advent was my inspiration, this book won't follow traditional Advent weeks, but it will follow the divinely inspired voices who whispered and shouted that salvation was coming.

Emory C. Hornaday

DECEMBER 1

*And I will put enmity between you and the
woman, and between your offspring and hers; he
will crush your head, and you will strike his heel.
Genesis 3:15*

Proto Evangelium

In the beginning God created
Let there be
Light
Let there be
Land and sea
Fish and fowl, flower and tree
The voice of the Creator
Vibrating
The light of the Son
Pulsating
The power of the Holy Spirit
Hovering
Let there be
Let there be
Let
There
Be
And it was
And it was good

But incomplete

Full of good things
But lacking something

Heaven waited with bated breath
As God scooped dirt
From the freshly created earth
And molded it into …
Could it be?
Was He really
Forming a figure reflective of
His own visage

And with a deep inhale
His lips kissed the dust of the earth
Exhaling the sacred breath of life
And in a blink the dust
Solidified, electrified, metamorphosized
Creator holding creation: Man

Ah yes, He said
This, this is Very Good

And very good it continued to be
So much in fact
From Man God created Woman
Two distinctly different
Yet equally representative
Of the Creator

He placed them in Eden
With just one instruction
This one tree right here
Don't eat of it
Everything else is yours
To consume as you see fit
All was well for a time
Woman and Man explored the land
Walking with their Creator
Hand in hand

Until one day when a slithering creature
Spoke, how odd,
And he asked them if
They'd really heard God
Did He really say
You can't eat of this tree?
He must be worried your
Eyes will open and see

See what, she asked?

Ah there are things you
Do not know
Things good and evil
And with a bite of this treat
You will be like Him,
Knowing it all

And with one swift pluck
She held the fruit that led to the fall
For the first time the world felt
Shame enter in
Their eyes were opened
As knowledge never intended to be released
Was realized

When the Creator entered the garden
He called out for His creation
They hid, unable to face
The One they disobeyed

The Creator called out for Man
Who, full of shame, replied
We are naked and afraid,
All we could think to do is hide

Who told you you were naked, Creator inquired

Did you eat of the tree that you were not supposed to eat from?
Woman gave it to me, Man accused
Creator turned to her, asking, what have you done?
The serpent gave it to me, she cried
Away the slithering creature attempted to slide, but
Creator unleashed His curse
A lifetime of groveling on his belly alone,
And enmity between it and she

Yet here is our first glimpse of Creator's plan
Before creation, before the fall,
He'd wisely prepared
A plan for us all
He knew He would need to provide a way
A path of redemption as mankind went astray

Where hostility hung thick between Woman and deceiver
In time, Love would overshadow another Woman
And she would bear the Deliverer
This deceiver would strike His heel,
But the Deliverer would crush his head

Christ, our Deliverer,
Would accomplish that task
When He died on the cross
Securing the keys of death and the grave
Resurrecting in glory that we may live ...

But first, He was promised to come
To be born as a babe
The Word made flesh
Making the way
For us to rejoin the Creator
In unity

Prophecy

And I will put enmity between you and the woman, and between your offspring and hers; he will crush your head, and you will strike his heel.
Genesis 3:15

Fulfillment

The one who does what is sinful is of the devil, because the devil has been sinning from the beginning. The reason the Son of God appeared was to destroy the devil's work.
1 John 3:8

And she gave birth to her firstborn, a son. She wrapped him in cloths and placed him in a manger, because there was no
guest room available for them.
Luke 2:7

But when the set time had fully come, God sent his Son, born of a woman, born under the law.
Galatians 4:4

Prayer

Father, thank you for the plan of redemption that you set in place before the creation of the world. Jesus has always been your plan for mankind to dwell in unity and connection with you. Thank you for sending Jesus as a man, and for his life, death, and resurrection which reconciled us to you. Amen.

Going Deeper

Why do you think God sent Jesus to the world as a baby?

Genesis 3:15 is the first prophecy in Scripture which reveals God's redemptive plan through Jesus. Have you read this verse as a prophecy before? What can we learn about the authority we have over evil from this verse?

Additional Study

Genesis 1–3

REFLECTIONS

DECEMBER 2

The Lord had said to Abram, "Leave your native country, your relatives, and your father's family, and go to the land that I will show you. I will make you into a great nation. I will bless you and make you famous, and you will be a blessing to others. I will bless those who bless you and curse those who treat you with contempt. All the families on earth will be blessed through you."
Genesis 12:1–3 (NLT)

The Blessing of Abraham

Where was Abram when he first heard
The voice of God call his name?
Was he strolling through the land,
Resting on a rock as he surveyed the beauty around him?
Was he leaving a time of fellowship with family
Or wrapping up the day's work to head home to Sarai?

The setting is a mystery
But if you will imagine with me:
An old man
One who yearned to be a father
Yet had no sons
One who carried the weight and shame of barrenness
Along with his wife
An old man who loved his nephew as if he was his own
An old man wondering what tomorrow may bring
Assuming more of the same
And as this old man ponders these things in his heart
While walking home to greet his wife
He hears a voice
In his head?
Out loud?
We do not know
But what he heard changed his quiet ponderings
Into possibilities
Leave your native land, your father's family and
Go to the land I will show you
I will make you into a great nation
I will bless you and you will bless others
All the families on earth will be blessed through you

In his shock, did that sting?
All families will be blessed through you,
One who has no heir
Or did it inspire hope?
I will make you a great nation
Many from the faith of one

Faith that believed the impossible
Was probable when the Divine intervened
This old man's faith became the gateway
Through which you and I are blessed
Not because of our bloodline,
But because one man chose to hope against hope
And believe that this Divine Force
Interrupting his life as he knew it
Was able to do what He promised

Abram followed the beckoning voice of the Lord
And set in motion
God's redemptive plan to bring blessing to
All families on the earth
Yet the wait for a son must've felt eternal
The yearning, the longing,
Getting the best of this couple trying to
Hold tightly to this promise, year after year
But they gave into fear, bearing a child
Through Sarai's servant
In Abram's eighty-sixth year
But he was not the heir God intended

Thirteen years trudge by and now Abram is ninety-nine
And once again God's voice breaks the barrier 'tween
Heaven and Earth
Affirming the promise made long before:
I will increase your numbers
As Abram falls flat on his face
God gives him a new name
Eternal father was good to begin with
Father of nations is how he would finish
Abram to Abraham, Sarai to Sarah
The breath of life exhaled into their identities
Creating the fruitfulness of one tiny baby

Though it took time
A great nation did indeed emerge
From Abraham's one son
Hundreds of generations later
All families on earth were blessed through Abraham's line
With the birth of the Promised One

Prophecy

The Lord had said to Abram, "Leave your native country, your relatives, and your father's family, and go to the land that I will show you. I will make you into a great nation. I will bless you and make you famous, and you will be a blessing to others. I will bless those who bless you and curse those who treat you with contempt. All the families on earth will be blessed through you."
Genesis 12:1–3 (NLT)

Fulfillment

You are the children of those prophets, and you are included in the covenant God promised to your ancestors. For God said to Abraham, "Through your descendants all the families on earth will be blessed." When God raised up his servant, Jesus, he sent him first to you people of Israel, to bless you by turning each of you back from your sinful ways.
Acts 3:25–26 (NLT)

Prayer

Thank you, Father, that with you all things are possible. Nothing is too hard for you! Whatever seemingly impossible situation I am facing today, I lay at your feet and ask you to intervene as only you can. Just as you answered the cry of Abram and Sarai's hearts, I trust you with the cry of mine. Amen.

Going Deeper

Genesis 12:3 says that all families on earth will be blessed through Abraham's line and Jesus is the ultimate fulfillment of this promise. Blessing is now available to all people because of His birth, death, and resurrection. We are able to see the big picture of this prophecy through the lens of time, but how do you think Abraham and Sarah understood this promise? How did they steward it?

What are promises that God has made you, and how are you stewarding them? Ask God if there is any way you can partner with what He is doing in your life today.

Additional Study

Genesis 12:1–9; Genesis 15:1–6; Genesis 16–17; Romans 4:17–25

REFLECTIONS

DECEMBER 3

*Then God said, "Yes, but your wife Sarah will
bear you a son, and you will call him Isaac. I will
establish my covenant with him as an everlasting
covenant for his descendants after him."*
Genesis 17:19

The Blessing of Isaac

Laughter
An appropriate name for a child of promise
What joy when disbelief dissolved into
Exuberant acknowledgment of life
Growing in a geriatric womb
Indeed the Divine had the last laugh as
He watched the two He'd chosen to parent nations
Celebrate their long awaited son

This son was special
He was set apart
The child of promise
For through him, the everlasting covenant
Would be confirmed

Like Abraham and Sarah
Israel too would wait
For a deliverer to break their chains

Some two thousand years later
Another Hebrew woman was told that
She would bear a son
Mary's soft reply:
Let it be as you have said
Not laughter, but willful acceptance of
The assignment before her
An assignment that could cost her everything
Her reputation
Her fiancé
Her hopes at ever being wed
Destined to be an outcast
All to bear
A special son who was
Set apart

A child of promise
Long awaited
For through Him, the everlasting covenant would be
Cut
Established
Paid for in blood and breath
So
Every chain would be broken
Every lie replaced with truth
And death defeated by life eternal

Sarah laughed in disbelief
When an angel prophesied her pregnancy
I wonder
If Mary laughed, too
As she held her newborn babe against her breast
A gentle, but victorious laugh
As she held close
The One anointed with the oil of gladness
Who would embody our sorrows
For the joy set before Him

Prophecy

Then God said, "Yes, but your wife Sarah will bear you a son, and you will call him Isaac. I will establish my covenant with him as an everlasting covenant for his descendants after him."
Genesis 17:19

Fulfillment

Nor because they are his descendants are they all Abraham's children. On the contrary, "It is through Isaac that your offspring will be reckoned."
Romans 9:7

Prayer

Thank you Father, for keeping your promises. You are a faithful God. Your word can be trusted. Though I may have laughed at the impossibility of what you've promised me, I know that you will come through for me.
Amen.

Going Deeper

Think of a promise that God has made you that feels laughable. Review Scripture and write down times that God brought impossible promises to pass. Read these Scriptures aloud to build your faith for what God wants to do for you.

Jesus was the most joyful person on the earth (Hebrews 1:9 notes that He was anointed with the oil of joy), and joy makes up a third of the Kingdom of God (Romans 14:17). In what ways can you enter into the river of joy available to you through Jesus, even if your circumstances are challenging? Look for ways to practice joy and engage in laughter as the holiday season begins.

Additional Study

Genesis 17; Genesis 18:1–15; Genesis 21:1–7; Luke 1:38; Hebrews 1:9

REFLECTIONS

DECEMBER 4

Your descendants will be like the dust of the earth, and you will spread out to the west and to the east, to the north and to the south. All peoples on earth will be blessed through you and your offspring.
Genesis 28:14

The Blessing of Jacob

Three generations of men
Three promises from the Most High
I will make you a great nation
An everlasting covenant with your descendants
They will be as the dust of the earth and
All people will be blessed through you and your offspring

The God of Abraham, Isaac, and Jacob
Making promises on a scale
Far grander than they could fathom
How could these three men who adventured
Through the Middle Eastern desert
Possibly know the promises given to them
Would find fulfillment in Divinity wrapped in flesh

I wonder, how Jacob thought about this promise:
All people will be blessed through you and your offspring
How many people was *all* to him,
What image did he see in his mind with the words *dust of the earth?*
How far to the east and west could he imagine?
Was there a cap on north and south in his mind?
Or could he look at the horizon and know
There was more beyond what he could see
How did he imagine blessing coming through him and his offspring?
Was it measured by bountiful harvests,
Ever increasing flocks, and children born?
Did this feel like an attaboy pat on the back from an unseen voice
Or did he feel the weight of the promise?

The Word made flesh chose this bloodline
To feed His umbilical cord
And as co-heirs with Christ, you and I are also infused
With the blessings of the forefathers

From Abraham we are fathered into faith
For his belief in God was credited as righteousness
He modeled hoping against hope
Believing for what couldn't have been reasonable
In this natural world
And that kind of faith is ours for the taking

Isaac gifts us the blessing of using our little for increase
For he sowed seed in a famine
And reaped one hundred times come harvest
So we too can use the little we have
And with the Lord's blessing
We shall see more come from less

Jacob invites us to receive God's divine solutions
For our earthly problems
Through dreams and encounters God guides Jacob
Revealing where he is to go
How to increase his flocks
And He even changes Jacob's name
To better reflect the promise on his life
So we too have access to the mind of Christ
Which releases heavenly wisdom
As we navigate bringing His Kingdom to Earth
According to the promise of Jacob
We have access to the blessing of prosperity, and a new name

All three lived imperfect lives,
Yet were weaved into the family tree of God
You are the dust of the earth from Genesis 28
You are blessed with faith, increase, divine solutions,
And a new name as a child of the King
Our forefathers waited,
Longing to see the fulfillment of a promise
Which did not come in their lifetime
But it has come in ours
We are living in the blessing they prayed for
And now, we must run the race marked out for us
So that together, these forerunners and their dust of the earth
May enter into the fullness of everything
That was paid for with
The birth, life, death, and resurrection of
The Promised Messiah

Prophecy

Your descendants will be like the dust of the earth, and you will spread out to the west and to the east, to the north and to the south. All peoples on earth will be blessed through you and your offspring.
Genesis 28:14

Fulfillment

... the son of Jacob, the son of Isaac, the son of Abraham, the son of Terah, the son of Nahor ...
Luke 3:34
Jacob is listed in the genealogy of Jesus.

Prayer

Thank you Father, that through our forefathers, Abraham, Isaac, and Jacob, we are blessed because you have brought your promises to them to pass in Christ. Thank you for access to hope and faith, prosperity despite our circumstances, and divine strategies and solutions for whatever we may face. You never stop providing and caring for your children. We bring our needs before you today, asking that you increase what we have sown, increase our faith for what you will do, and release solutions from Heaven so that we may see your Kingdom come here on Earth. Amen.

Going Deeper

Romans 4:3 tells us that Abraham's faith was credited to him as righteousness, and verses 23 and 24 state, "The words 'it was credited to him' were written not for him alone, but also for us, to whom God will credit righteousness—for us who believe in him who raised Jesus our Lord from the dead." God credits our faith in Jesus as righteousness, hallelujah!

In what area of your life would you like to increase your faith? Ask God to increase your faith in the area you've chosen. Write down what you'd like to see in this area, and commit to praying for it for the next month or two. After that time, journal how your faith has grown regarding this situation.

Hebrews 11:6 tells us that faith is pleasing to God and that He is a rewarder of those who seek Him; consider meditating on that verse for encouragement.

First Corinthians 2:16 says that "we have the mind of Christ," so we can ask Him for guidance and solutions knowing that He desires to share His thoughts with us. Bring your requests before Him today, in confidence that the God of Jacob will guide you.

Additional Study

Genesis 28:10–22; Romans 4:17–25; Genesis 26:1–6; 12–13; Genesis 30:25–43; Genesis 32:22–32; 1 Corinthians 2:16b; Hebrews 11:39–12:1

REFLECTIONS

DECEMBER 5

The scepter will not depart from Judah, nor the ruler's staff from between his feet, until he to whom it belongs shall come and the obedience of the nations shall be his.
Genesis 49:10

The Scepter of Judah

Only God would call forth a king
From the line of an irresponsible rebel
Fourth son of Jacob, born of an unloved wife
Sibling rivalry, asserting for dominance,
Choosing rebellion, how'd it all begin?

Judah conspired with his brothers to take down
Joseph, the son their father loved most
The brothers wanted to take Joseph's life
But Judah saw no gain in death
And with his next breath said, let's sell him
The brothers agreed and after negotiations
Joseph was traded for some coin
And Judah and his brothers let their father
Believe he was dead and gone

Judah became a man so entwined with sin that it took
Coming face to face with the
Daughter-in-law he unknowingly impregnated
For him to see how far he'd fallen
And now—twins
Who needed a father who could hold it together
And make their life better
Than the life he'd been leading

While we don't know the ins and outs
Of Judah's next steps
We do see in Genesis 43
That Judah, the fourth-born
Steps up like he's the firstborn
And offers his own life as security
For the safe return of his little brother Benji

You see there was a famine in the land and
The second in command of Egypt said
He'd give no more grain to the family
Without seeing for himself that they had a little brother
Their daddy Jacob said oh no
I've already lost one son from my beloved wife
I can't bear to lose another

But Judah guaranteed his brother's safety
And Jacob finally relented
The whole family was hungry
Off they went to see this man with such
A strange request
And upon arrival there was a little dinner party
Which seemed a bit odd to the brothers, but
It'd be rude to turn down food
Especially when it's scarce where they came from

The next day there was some drama
About a stolen cup
Which was a set up
But Judah didn't know that yet
So he took the lead and
Made his plea for the safe
Return of little Benji and
Then to his astonishment
His other little brother Joseph
Revealed he was alive and well
And the family was reunited

Pharaoh insisted that the whole family
Move to town
So as old as he was
Jacob packed his boxes and traveled south
He settled in surrounded by
His next of kin
And started blessing them one by one
And when he got to Judah, his wayward son
He identified him as the man he had become
A lion, a ruler, deserving of honor
And a seat on the throne
He prophesied as his life was passing by:
The scepter will not leave you
Until the coming of the one it belongs to

If you follow Judah's line
You'll find
One son after another
Including Boaz, Jesse, David, Solomon
But that's not the end
Generations later this rebel's legacy
Turned into the royal family tree
When Jesus Christ was born
And stepped into His destiny as
King of Judah
Bearer of the Scepter

Judah is proof that a rebel
Can change his ways
And walk in grace
Establishing a legacy
That rules and reigns

Prophecy

The scepter will not depart from Judah, nor the ruler's staff from between his feet, until he to whom it belongs shall come and the obedience of the nations shall be his.
Genesis 49:10

Fulfillment

... the son of Amminadab, the son of Ram, the son of Hezron, the son of Perez, the son of Judah ...
Luke 3:33
Judah is listed in the genealogy of Jesus.

Prayer

Father, thank you for second, third, and fourth chances. Thank you for the forgiveness that comes through Christ and enables me to start over. No matter who I have been in the past, you can turn things around. Thank you for saving me, and for showing me how to follow you so that I can leave a legacy of faith to my family and friends. Amen.

Going Deeper

Why do you think Jesus's family line is filled with those who've made mistakes? What do you think God is saying by including people like Judah?

What kind of legacy do you want to leave for your family and friends? What, if any, changes can you make today that will help you achieve the legacy you're wanting to leave?

Additional Study

Genesis 37–38; 42–45; 49:8–12

REFLECTIONS

DECEMBER 6

The Lord declares to you that the Lord himself will establish a house for you: When your days are over and you rest with your ancestors, I will raise up your offspring to succeed you, your own flesh and blood, and I will establish his kingdom. He is the one who will build a house for my Name, and I will establish the throne of his kingdom forever.... Your house and your kingdom will endure forever before me; your throne will be established forever.
2 Samuel 7:11–13, 16

The Throne of David

David
A man after God's own heart
A shepherd boy who beat the odds and
Rose above his brothers in his bloodline
To be anointed as the king to come

The boy who dropped off some bread and cheese
To his brothers on the front lines
Only to pick up a stone and take on a giant on the battlefield
For defying the God of Israel
He prophesied success
And in seconds
The giant was laid out and headless

The courage of a boy who'd fought private battles
Thrust this young man into the public eye
His renown began to spread in such a way that
The current king soon wanted him dead

A fugitive among his own people
Far from the throne he was anointed for
David gathered man after man until
An army of mighty men was formed
And he took land, defended his people,
Righteously ruled those who followed him
Acting like the king he was called to be
Long before the crown graced his head

And when he finally acceded his throne
He dove into worshiping the King above all kings
He insisted on bringing the Holy of Holies into the streets
So everyone could worship the Presence of the Most High
He worshiped so freely he embarrassed his wife
By dancing half naked where all could see

Now, he was not a man without fault,
Adultery and murder marked him, but
Humility and repentance marked him more and
David was a man who knew what it was to be forgiven much

And those who have been forgiven know how to worship
David wanted nothing more than to build a house for God
But God had other plans
The Father decreed:
I will build a house for you instead, your house
And your kingdom will continue forever before me,
And your throne will endure forever

With that, God secured David in His family tree
And in Matthew chapter one we read the genealogy
Of Jesus the Messiah, descendant of David

Prophecy

The Lord declares to you that the Lord himself will establish a house for you: When your days are over and you rest with your ancestors, I will raise up your offspring to succeed you, your own flesh and blood, and I will establish his kingdom. He is the one who will build a house for my Name, and I will establish the throne of his kingdom forever.... Your house and your kingdom will endure forever before me; your throne will be established forever.
2 Samuel 7:11–13, 16

Fulfillment

This is the genealogy of Jesus the Messiah the son of David, the son of Abraham.
Matthew 1:1

Prayer

Father, thank you for showing us through the lineage of Jesus that there is hope for the lost, broken, and rebellious to find their way home. You see the motives of my heart and know me intimately. I pray that, like David, I would operate in great faith and live a life of worship unto you. In moments of failure, Lord help me to be humble and quick to repent.
May I never take your forgiveness for granted. Thank you for the example of David who had a heart after yours. Mold my heart to be after yours as well. Amen.

Going Deeper

In what ways was David "a man after God's own heart?"
How was his life a type of Christ?

The psalms of David are full of prophecies about Jesus. Read through one or more of the references below and look up the New Testament fulfillment. Ponder the fact that David had the honor of prophesying into his legacy, and consider how you can speak into your future family today.
Psalm 2:1–2; Psalm 22:15–16, 18; Psalm 34:20; Psalm 89:3–4; Psalm 110:1

Additional Study

1 Samuel 16–17; 27; 2 Samuel 6; 11–12:23

REFLECTIONS

DECEMBER 7

The Lord your God will raise up for you a prophet like me from among you, from your fellow Israelites. You must listen to him.
Deuteronomy 18:15

A Prophet Like Moses

This prophecy of Christ's birth
Precedes Isaiah's verse
Before *unto us a child is born* was penned
The first prophet of God's people decreed:
A prophet like me will come from among you

You see, God's invitation was for His people to draw near
That all may hear His voice and know Him intimately
But the fear of God misapplied
Led to their request not to hear His voice or
See His fire for fear of death
Lord, let there be a mediator
Someone to go between
A request He granted, though it was Plan B
Moses was selected and faithfully served
And God allowed this mediator prophet
As a sign of His Plan A

A prophet like me will come from among you
But with the promise of this new prophet
Comes the key:
You must listen
And from Mt. Sinai God confirms
I will put my words in His mouth
And He will speak for me

But did they receive?
Did they partner with the prophecy
Applying their belief?
Surely none would have imagined
The many genealogies
That would die and breathe life
Before the Prophet like Moses
Parted the veil

Moses was the prophet
To whom God revealed
The fullness of His glory
The one He spoke to as a friend
The narrator of the beginning of His-story
He spoke with God face to face

And I wonder if God missed those conversations
If His plan of redemption stemmed
From missing this connection with men
Perhaps face to face simply wasn't enough
And He wanted a hug
To hold His creation to His chest
So they could find peace and rest

Ultimately, I believe, He wanted to restore their dignity
To remove the need for a middle man
And reinstate His original plan
Where everyone has the ability to hear His voice
And encounter Him without fear of death, but immersed in Love

Jesus fulfilled these words of Moses
By becoming the final middle man
The last and greatest sacrifice
The Way the Truth the Life
He only spoke what the Lord was saying
And He made a way to open our ears and eyes
So you and I may see and hear God too

Face to face, Father and Son commune
Just like God did with Moses
And now … so can you
Jesus, the image of the invisible God
Brought us back into God's Presence
His words are life, and we now hold the key
To tune our ear to the Father's voice
And in reverential awe, listen
For what He will whisper to you and to me

Prophecy

The Lord your God will raise up for you a prophet like me from among you, from your fellow Israelites. You must listen to him.
Deuteronomy 18:15

Fulfillment

The God of Abraham, Isaac and Jacob, the God of our fathers, has glorified his servant Jesus ... For Moses said, "The Lord your God will raise up for you a prophet like me from among your own people; you must listen to everything he tells you. Anyone who does not listen to him will be completely cut off from their people."
Acts 3:13, 22–23

Prayer

Thank you, Father, that you created us for connection with you! Thank you, Jesus, for coming to Earth and becoming like us, so that you could be the perfect mediator. Your birth, life, death, and resurrection has made a way for me to have access to God, you, and Holy Spirit at all times. I am so thankful that you live in me and I in you. Amen.

Going Deeper

Read Exodus 20:18–21, Deuteronomy 18:15–18, and Proverbs 9:10. What is the fear of the Lord? What do you think is the proper application of the fear of the Lord?

Read Matthew 27:50–51.
What did the tearing of the veil symbolize?

Additional Study

Exodus 20:18–21; 33:11–23; John 12:49–50; 14:6; Colossians 1:15

REFLECTIONS

DECEMBER 8

I will raise up for myself a faithful priest, who will do according to what is in my heart and mind. I will firmly establish his priestly house, and they will minister before my anointed one always.
1 Samuel 2:35

A Faithful Priest

Life is in the blood
And blood the sign of sacrifice

The priests of the day slaughtered
Bulls and goats, lambs and birds
For the forgiveness of sins

As we read Leviticus from our
Comfortable quiet-time chairs
We can hardly fathom the
Sight and smell of sticky, metallic blood that
Splattered, dripped, and drained through the temple courts

How could it be that a goat
Could die for me?
That his perfect young body
Could be offered up in place of
The lie that was told, the apple I stole,
The cruel words I spoke, the deceit I undertook?

And year after year, on the day of atonement
All of Israel gathered to bestow upon one goat
The sins of the nation
And upon another
The nation's rebellion

One was slaughtered, its blood spattered,
Its body burnt, making atonement for sin
So God can enter into
The Holy of Holies and commune
With His people

The other released into the wilderness
Carrying the weight of the people on its back
A scapegoat, exiled

Year after year,
Rivers of blood flowed through the Temple
Yet there was a promise of a new day coming
I will raise up for myself a faithful priest
There will be one who will serve perfectly
As the great high priest
But who is worthy?

For He must be perfect in every way, blameless
He will be despised and rejected
Suffering will define him, and pain will be a familiar friend
Indeed Isaiah says that he will take on our pain
And our suffering
He will be pierced, crushed, punished
Oppressed and afflicted,
Chastised for sins he did not commit
In bearing the weight of the sins of all humanity
For now and time to come,
He becomes our great intercessor, pouring His life out
The perfect, once-and-for-all blood sacrifice
Who now lives to intercede on our behalf
And whose blood covers us in righteousness
Allowing us to boldly enter the throne room
With confidence
For those who accept this ultimate sacrifice
Join the royal priesthood
Under the Faithful Priest, Jesus

Prophecy

I will raise up for myself a faithful priest, who will do according to what is in my heart and mind. I will firmly establish his priestly house, and they will minister before my anointed one always.
1 Samuel 2:35

Fulfillment

For this reason he had to be made like them, fully human in every way, in order that he might become a merciful and faithful high priest in service to God, and that he might make atonement for the sins of the people.
Hebrews 2:17

Prayer

Jesus, thank you for fulfilling the role of faithful priest. Because you, the Son of God, came into this world like us, you perfectly fulfilled the roles of both priest and sacrifice. This made a way for me to connect directly with the Father, you, and Holy Spirit without a mediator. I am so grateful to have a way to connect with you, any time of day or night. Amen.

Going Deeper

Why was a faithful priest an integral part of God's redemption plan?

This devotional is influenced by several passages in Scripture. Meditate on these passages and dialogue with God about His intricate redemption plan:

> For the life of a creature is in the blood, and I have given it to you to make atonement for yourselves on the altar; it is the blood that makes atonement for one's life.
> Leviticus 17:11

> First he said, "Sacrifices and offerings, burnt offerings and sin offerings you did not desire, nor were you pleased with them"—though they were offered in accordance with the law. Then he said, "Here I am, I have come to do your will." He sets aside the first to establish the second. And by that will, we have been made holy through the sacrifice of the body of Jesus Christ once for all. Day after day every priest stands and performs his religious duties; again and again he offers the same sacrifices, which can never take away sins. But when this priest had offered for all time one sacrifice for sins, he sat down at the right hand of God, and since that time he waits for his enemies to be made his footstool. For by one sacrifice he has made perfect forever those who are being made holy.
> Hebrews 10:8–14

Who has believed our message and to whom has the arm of the Lord been revealed? He grew up before him like a tender shoot, and like a root out of dry ground. He had no beauty or majesty to attract us to him, nothing in his appearance that we should desire him. He was despised and rejected by mankind, a man of suffering, and familiar with pain. Like one from whom people hide their faces he was despised, and we held him in low esteem. Surely he took up our pain and bore our suffering, yet we considered him punished by God, stricken by him, and afflicted. But he was pierced for our transgressions, he was crushed for our iniquities; the punishment that brought us peace was on him, and by his wounds we are healed. We all, like sheep, have gone astray, each of us has turned to our own way; and the Lord has laid on him the iniquity of us all. He was oppressed and afflicted, yet he did not open his mouth; he was led like a lamb to the slaughter, and as a sheep before its shearers is silent, so he did not open his mouth. By oppression and judgment he was taken away. Yet who of his generation protested? For he was cut off from the land of the living; for the transgression of my people he was punished. He was assigned a grave with the wicked, and with the rich in his death, though he had done no violence, nor was any deceit in his mouth. Yet it was the Lord's will to crush him and cause him to suffer, and though the Lord makes his life an offering for sin, he will see his offspring and prolong his days, and the will of the Lord will prosper in his hand. After he has suffered, he will see the light of life and be satisfied; by his knowledge my righteous servant will justify many, and he will bear their iniquities. Therefore I will give him a portion among the great, and he will divide the spoils with the strong, because he poured out his life unto death, and was numbered with the transgressors. For he bore the sin of many, and made intercession for the transgressors.

Isaiah 53

REFLECTIONS

DECEMBER 9

The Lord reigns forever; he has established his throne for judgment. He rules the world in righteousness and judges the peoples with equity. The Lord is a refuge for the oppressed, a stronghold in times of trouble. Those who know your name trust in you, for you, Lord, have never forsaken those who seek you.
Psalm 9:7–10

A Just Judge

Yeshua, the One Who Saves
Jesus came not as a judge, but as Savior
We all know John 3:16
But verse seventeen rings clear
He came not to condemn the world
But that through Him, the world might be saved
Jesus, the great redemption plan from the foundation

Yet, throughout Scripture we see glimpses
Of the heavenly organization the Father has set in place
He designed a court system in the spirit realm
Our enemy is known as the Accuser
Tempting our thoughts into doubt and fear
Dragging our every wayward word before the throne
As evidence held against us

But we have a Mediator, One who stands in our place,
Pleading our case to the Father
And because of His sacrifice,
We are clothed in white
Seen as if we were Jesus Himself

Our Advocate defends us before the Accuser
And nothing he brings forward
Will stand a chance in this courtroom

The incarnation was for our salvation
However
Because Jesus, who was, and is, and will ever be
Laid down His divinity and lived as a man
He is more than a Savior,
He was our final Mediator and now is
The perfect and just judge for all mankind

His judgment for believers, based on how we
Lived our lives once we received the gift of Christ,
Will be for our reward
As He separates the sheep who know His voice
From those who called Him Lord, yet never knew Him

His justice is pure and complete
His judgment reserved for a day to come
Oh how gracious of the Father to bring forth a Son
Who crossed the divide, that expanse of holy divinity
And shrugged on skin, constraining Himself to life within
Flesh and bone, blood and tendon
Who lived like us, loved us, knowing our full experience
And died for us that we may sit before the Bema Seat
Clean

Prophecy

The Lord reigns forever; he has established his throne for judgment. He rules the world in righteousness and judges the peoples with equity. The Lord is a refuge for the oppressed, a stronghold in times of trouble. Those who know your name trust in you, for you, Lord, have never forsaken those who seek you.
Psalm 9:7–10

Fulfillment

For he has set a day when he will judge the world with justice by the man he has appointed. He has given proof of this to everyone by raising him from the dead.
Acts 17:31

Prayer

Jesus, our perfect judge! Your judgment is not for our condemnation, but for our reward! Because you are perfect and righteous in every way, your justice and judgments are as well. Help me to steward what you've entrusted me with in a way that brings you the most honor and glory. Thank you that this stewardship leads to reward. You are as generous as you are just! Amen.

Going Deeper

Read John 5:19–23, focusing on verse 22, and John 9:39. Why do you think the Father entrusted judgment to the Son?

Read 2 Corinthians 5:10. As you think about the judgment seat of Christ, often called the Bema Seat, why do you think Jesus is the one sitting in that seat, instead of the Father or Holy Spirit? What uniquely qualifies Jesus for this role of just judge?

Additional Study

Psalm 82:1 (NLT); John 3:16–17; 14:16–17; Hebrews 12:24; 1 John 2:1; Revelation 12:10

REFLECTIONS

DECEMBER 10

But you, Bethlehem Ephrathah, though you are small among the clans of Judah, out of you will come for me one who will be ruler over Israel, whose origins are from of old, from ancient times.
Micah 5:2

Born In Bethlehem

The prophet Micah declared
That out of the small town of Bethlehem
A ruler over Israel would come
When eyes would be turned to Jerusalem
The seat of power, the city of troops
A city ready to welcome the ruler of a nation
The prophet turns our attention to
A small town further south
An unlikely locale

The birthplace of David
A city known as the House of Bread
Little did anyone know
The Christ Child born there
Would turn the world on its head
Rachel's tomb nearby
Pastureland as far as the eye can see
Not quite as developed as cities up north
But since when does God do anything
Like we think He should

Significance out of insignificance
Greatness out of that which is the least
Isn't that just like God?
He has a way of taking something unassuming
That has been dismissed, set aside, discarded,
And choosing to raise it up high

He seems to have a thing for the least of these
The lowly, the humble,
Those that are bumbling their way through
Which, personally I'm quite grateful for, aren't you?
Instead of going for the obvious strategy,
Raising up a military power to rescue this land,
His plan was much more involved
A global rescue, you might say
One that was prophesied throughout our Holy Scriptures
And while Bethlehem may have been considered the least
God's eye was on that land, and according to His plan
It was the perfect location to introduce the babe that would
One day rule every nation, tribe, and tongue

Out of the House of Bread
Came the Bread of Life
Insignificant land
Yielding significance

This prophecy fulfilled invites us to self-examination
What have we dismissed, set aside,
Or discarded about ourselves
That may be the very location of
New life and fruitfulness
Nothing is insignificant to His eye
Allow Him to highlight
That which you may have overlooked within yourself
And invite Him to bring significance

Prophecy

But you, Bethlehem Ephrathah, though you are small among the clans of Judah, out of you will come for me one who will be ruler over Israel, whose origins are from of old, from ancient times.
Micah 5:2

Fulfillment

When he had called together all the people's chief priests and teachers of the law, he asked them where the Messiah was to be born. "In Bethlehem in Judea," they replied, "for this is what the prophet has written: 'But you, Bethlehem, in the land of Judah, are by no means least among the rulers of Judah; for out of you will come a ruler who will shepherd my people Israel.'"
Matthew 2:4–6

So Joseph also went up from the town of Nazareth in Galilee to Judea, to Bethlehem the town of David, because he belonged to the house and line of David. He went there to register with Mary, who was pledged to be married to him and was expecting a child. While they were there, the time came for the baby to be born, and she gave birth to her firstborn, a son. She wrapped him in cloths and placed him in a manger, because there was no guest room available for them.
Luke 2:4–7

Prayer

Father, thank you that you are a God who infuses significance in all areas of our lives. Just as you chose a small town for the birth of your Son, you are also aware of the small things in my life. Today I bring to you the things that have felt too insignificant to talk about, and I also ask that you examine me for any area that I've overlooked where you want to bring significance in my life. Amen.

Going Deeper

The people of Israel were expecting their salvation to come through a military power who would overthrow the Romans. Why do you think God sent Jesus as a baby who grew up as an apprentice to his earthly father instead of introducing Him into the world as an adult?

Why do you think where Jesus was born was included in prophecy? Is there anyone in Scripture that referenced this verse in Micah? (Hint: read Matthew 2:1–12.)

Additional Study

Matthew 25:40; John 6:35

REFLECTIONS

DECEMBER 11

*When Israel was a child, I loved him,
and out of Egypt I called my son.
Hosea 11:1*

Out Of Egypt

When Israel was a child, I loved him,
And out of Egypt I called my son

Hosea hearkens us back to
The beginning of God's beloved people
The family of Jacob
Relocated to a foreign land
All a part of God's grand plan
But before long this small family
Grew to an impressive nation of its own
And in fear, the Pharaoh of the day
Shackled and chained Jacob's sons
Until not a one recalled the feel of freedom

But God heard their cries, their sighs,
Their pleas for justice, for release
And He raised up a redeemer
Who met Pharaoh face to face and demanded
That his people be let go
The fullness of this story is worth its own telling
But for now, let us focus in on that moment when
Millions of Hebrew men, women, and children
Laid down their chains and crossed the boundary line from
Slavery into freedom

Out of Egypt, God called His beloved people Israel
As a master storyteller, it's no surprise
To see Him weave in a reprise
To this foundational moment in history
Aligning His beloved Son Jesus with
His beloved people Israel
He sends an angel in a dream to Joseph
Telling him to flee to Egypt
As King Herod is executing all young sons
So Jesus spends his toddler years
In the land of His people's slavery
And just as Moses led Israel to freedom
Promising a prophet greater than he would come
So Jesus, the Redeemer of all mankind
Fulfills that promise, and at the death of Herod
Joseph receives another dream
Come, out of Egypt
Return home with my Son

Prophecy

When Israel was a child, I loved him, and out of Egypt I called my son.
Hosea 11:1

Fulfillment

So he got up, took the child and his mother during the night and left for Egypt, where he stayed until the death of Herod. And so was fulfilled what the Lord had said through the prophet: "Out of Egypt I called my son."
Matthew 2:14–15

Prayer

Thank you that you are a God who always provides a way. You are more faithful to us than we can fathom. Thank you, Jesus, for coming as my Redeemer, showing me the way out of all that held me captive. Amen.

Going Deeper

Consider your personal testimony—in what ways has Jesus helped you out of your "Egypt?"

Why do you think this was a prophecy God wanted to see made and fulfilled? How does it add to the metanarrative of the salvation story?

Additional Study

Genesis 45:16–28; 46; Exodus 1; 3; 5–14; Matthew 2

REFLECTIONS

DECEMBER 12

Again the Lord spoke to Ahaz, "Ask the Lord your God for a sign, whether in the deepest depths or in the highest heights." But Ahaz said, "I will not ask; I will not put the Lord to the test." Then Isaiah said, "Hear now, you house of David! Is it not enough to try the patience of humans? Will you try the patience of my God also? Therefore the Lord himself will give you a sign: The virgin will conceive and give birth to a son, and will call him Immanuel."
Isaiah 7:10–14

The Impossible Sign

Has the Lord ever asked you
To ask Him for an impossible sign?
A sign that couldn't be missed
A giant billboard, addressed to you
Clearly stating … This is your sign!

We often desire such signs
I've asked for God to write on my mirror
To send me a text message
Anything so that I could be sure
That I'm sure
That I'm hearing Him

But Ahaz refused to ask for a sign
Even after God told him to ask for one,
And to make it impossible

Doesn't that sound just like God?
After all, He specializes in impossible,
So asking for a sign that's likely to happen
Is a tad insulting to the Great I AM

Yet here we are, with a stubborn, idolatrous king
About to lose his kingdom to warring factions,
Trying to broker a deal with an ungodly nation for protection
Rather than turning to the God of his people

So God sends the prophet Isaiah
With the message that Judah would not be overcome
Ahaz's kingdom would be victorious
Because the LORD would make it so
But, He commands Ahaz to ask Him for a sign
Oh, and by the way, make it impossible
For a sign confirms the word

Upon the king's refusal to test God
(Though is it really testing when God tells you to do it?)
Isaiah released the sign anyway, saying
The Lord Himself will give you this sign!
This impossible, improbable, seemingly ridiculous sign that

A virgin will conceive
And give birth
And call His name Immanuel, God with us

There is more to the prophecy
But a *virgin will conceive*
Well that is quite the impossibility

Digging deeply into these ancient texts
Reveals an interesting interpretation
The Hebrew of Isaiah 7
Translates "virgin" as "a woman of marrying age"
And Isaiah 8 clearly outlines the fulfillment of this word
Through Isaiah and his wife's own child

However,
Matthew in his intentionally specific language
Quotes Isaiah 7:14 using the Greek word for virgin
So this prophecy was both near and far,
Fulfilled for Ahaz, and also left vibrating in the airwaves
Awaiting the one whom God favored to carry His holy seed

I've heard it said that signs confirm the spoken word
And signs point us to God Himself
And in this case, this impossible sign did just that
It confirmed the word to a fearful king
And pointed every Israelite's eyes far into the future
As they awaited the virgin who would carry
God with us

Prophecy

Again the Lord spoke to Ahaz, "Ask the Lord your God for a sign, whether in the deepest depths or in the highest heights." But Ahaz said, "I will not ask; I will not put the Lord to the test." Then Isaiah said, "Hear now, you house of David! Is it not enough to try the patience of humans? Will you try the patience of my God also? Therefore the Lord himself will give you a sign: The virgin will conceive and give birth to a son, and will call him Immanuel."
Isaiah 7:10–14

Fulfillment

This is how the birth of Jesus the Messiah came about: His mother Mary was pledged to be married to Joseph, but before they came together, she was found to be pregnant through the Holy Spirit. Because Joseph her husband was faithful to the law, and yet did not want to expose her to public disgrace, he had in mind to divorce her quietly. But after he had considered this, an angel of the Lord appeared to him in a dream and said, "Joseph son of David, do not be afraid to take Mary home as your wife, because what is conceived in her is from the Holy Spirit. She will give birth to a son, and you are to give him the name Jesus, because he will save his people from their sins." All this took place to fulfill what the Lord had said through the prophet: "The virgin will conceive and give birth to a son, and they will call him Immanuel" (which means "God with us").
Matthew 1:18–23

Prayer

Nothing is impossible with you! I lay everything that seems to be impossible at your feet today, knowing that you can specialize in making the impossible possible. Thank you for giving such a beautiful sign so many years ago that points me to Jesus, and reveals the kind of God that you are. I am in awe of you, Lord. Amen

Going Deeper

Do you have a testimony of something impossible that God has done for you? Take time to write it down today with as much detail as possible, then share it with a friend or someone who would be encouraged by it.

What other impossible things did God do in Scripture? As you study the Bible, keep a journal of those miraculous acts. When you face a challenging situation, refer to that list and ask God to do what He did back then in the situation you're facing now.

Additional Study

Isaiah 7–8; Matthew 1:22–23

REFLECTIONS

DECEMBER 13

Therefore the Lord himself will give you a sign: The virgin will conceive and give birth to a son, and will call him Immanuel.
Isaiah 7:14

God With Us

*A virgin will conceive
And give birth
And call His name Immanuel, God with us*

Isaiah's prophecy took 700 years to come to fruition
But Luke tells us of Mary, a young woman
Perhaps fourteen or fifteen years old
Who was favored by God

Can you imagine what it felt like
To have Gabriel appear before you?
To be in the presence of a being
Who radiates with the holiness of God?
And how does a teenager, betrothed, not yet married
Grapple with the news that she will become pregnant and
Not only carry, but also raise, the Savior,
The Messiah that her people had longed for?

Oh that I may be like Mary in my responses to the Lord
When He favors me with an assignment!
I am your servant, may your word to me be fulfilled

And the Holy Spirit came upon her
And the power of the Mighty One overshadowed her
And immediately an embryo
Began to grow within her
God in her becoming
God with us

Immanuel … the infinite impossibly becoming finite
Through the impossible conception of
The Divine overshadowing Its own creation
The humility of the Word in the beginning with God
Becoming a babe
Who could not speak or crawl
But only cry and sleep

God … who was before "In the Beginning"
Who created everything we know and experience
By simply speaking it into being
Who is not only Creator but Sustainer,
Almighty, All Powerful, Most Holy,
Majesty, Pure Wonder, the very essence of Love

With … Together
Side by side, inhabit, tabernacled,
Connected, intersected, fully woven
I in You and You in me

Us
Me
You
Them
Yes, them too

He is with us all, and to those that have received Him,
He is with you and in you, and you are also in Him
What captivating mystery of divine union
Immanuel—God has come to us

Prophecy

Therefore the Lord himself will give you a sign: The virgin will conceive and give birth to a son, and will call him Immanuel.
Isaiah 7:14

Fulfillment

This is how the birth of Jesus the Messiah came about: His mother Mary was pledged to be married to Joseph, but before they came together, she was found to be pregnant through the Holy Spirit. Because Joseph her husband was faithful to the law, and yet did not want to expose her to public disgrace, he had in mind to divorce her quietly. But after he had considered this, an angel of the Lord appeared to him in a dream and said, "Joseph son of David, do not be afraid to take Mary home as your wife, because what is conceived in her is from the Holy Spirit. She will give birth to a son, and you are to give him the name Jesus, because he will save his people from their sins." All this took place to fulfill what the Lord had said through the prophet: "The virgin will conceive and give birth to a son, and they will call him Immanuel" (which means "God with us").
Matthew 1:18–23

I am the true vine, and my Father is the gardener …
Remain in me, as I also remain in you.
John 15:1, 4a

Prayer

What a gift to never be without you, Jesus! I am in you and you are in me. Thank you for the promise that you will never leave or forsake me, but you walk with me each moment. Today I want to rest in your nearness, abiding in you as you move through me to love and serve others. Amen.

Going Deeper

When you hear that God will never leave you or forsake you, how does that make you feel? Journal about a time when you knew He was near. Just as the mystery of the Father, Son, and Holy Spirit being three in one is beyond our full comprehension, so too is our divine union with Christ through abiding. Yet, by faith, we can believe in what we do not understand.

As you contemplate union with Christ, how do you see Him in you, and you in Him?

Additional Study

Isaiah 7; Luke 1:26–38; Genesis 1; Colossians 1:17

REFLECTIONS

DECEMBER 14

*For to us a child is born, to us a son is given,
and the government will be on his shoulders.*
Isaiah 9:6a

The Weight Of Authority

There's a whole theological meaning behind this verse
That a poem won't do justice
So if you'll indulge me
Let's look at this more literally
When I hear that the government will be on His shoulders
I understand it means authority
But what I see is Jesus
With the White House on one shoulder,
Parliament across His back,
Tribal chieftains wrapped around His neck

All the seats of executive, legal, and judicial
That exist in the world
Engulfing Christ

Can you imagine carrying that weight?

Every administration, policy, legality
Each one defining the reality in which we exist
How does one man carry that?
How can He be so present as to tune in and
Dedicate His time to the affairs of all the world?

For Him, time isn't a thing
He sits outside it
Making Him a perfect candidate
To see the end from the beginning and
Guide those of us within it
And rest assured,
He is dedicated to our affairs
Because He paid the ultimate price for us
And He cares how things play out so
Despite what some may tell you
He's paying attention and actively involved
In our day-to-day lives

I think He gets a bit tickled at our attempts
To separate church and state
Since His idea of church is
Living inside of those of us who receive Him
While we go about being citizens seeking to bring
The goodness and light of a greater Kingdom

I know *government* isn't really what this verse is about
But this is what it makes me think of
A perfect king, president, lawyer, judge, chief, royal, ruler
The only hope we have for unity
In Him there are differences without division
Personality without pride
Commandments obeyed through love and not control
Truth that quiets every lie
Every conspiracy must bend the knee
To the One whose light makes all plain to see
But right now, we're talking about a baby
Entering the world with soft cries and tears in His eyes
For unto us a child is born
Whose tender shoulders would bear
The greatest measure of authority

Prophecy

For to us a child is born, to us a son is given,
and the government will be on his shoulders.
Isaiah 9:6a

Fulfillment

Then Jesus came to them and said,
"All authority in heaven and on earth has been given to me."
Matthew 28:18

Prayer

Jesus, it's hard to think of you coming as a baby, yet with such massive responsibility placed upon you. Only you are able to bear the weight of what is on your shoulders. Thank you for being the perfect executor of the government of the Kingdom. As I celebrate the joy of your coming, I hold in tension the weight of why you came, and in gratitude, I praise you.
Amen.

Going Deeper

It's possible the Israelites understood this prophecy in Isaiah to mean that the Savior would be a military or political figure. Why do you think God sent Jesus as a servant, instead?

What you are carrying may not be the weight of the world, but it's a weight nonetheless. Isaiah 9:6, and the cross, show us the weight that Jesus's shoulders can bear. As you sit with Him today, write down that which is weighing you down and then close your eyes and imagine these things resting on His capable shoulders. Read Matthew 11:28–30, thanking Him for all that He can carry on your behalf.

Additional Study

John 15:1–7; Colossians 1:27

REFLECTIONS

DECEMBER 15

For to us a child is born, to us a son is given, and the government will be on his shoulders. And he will be called Wonderful Counselor, Mighty God, Everlasting Father, Prince of Peace.
Isaiah 9:6

Wonderful, Counselor

The refrain of Handel's *Messiah* rings in my ears
Wonderful
Counselor
Almighty God
Everlasting Father
Have you noticed the pause
Between wonderful and counselor?
I wonder if that is intentional
While widely accepted to be companions
An adjective to a noun
I've often wondered if these may be two titles

Wonderful

If I had bouquets upon bouquets of flowers full of petals
I'd run out before I could count the ways
Indeed all the grains of sand on the earth
Cannot number the vastness of His wonder
By virtue of this title He is indeed full of wonder itself
My mind can hardly begin to theorize, imagine, construe how to define
What the fullness of wonder attempts to encapsulate
The only word that does it justice
The only word that emanates
Is His very name
A name so wonderful knees bow before Him
Hands and faces lie prostrate on the floor crying out for more of this
Wonderful Divine Being
Who shed His divinity and entered humanity through conception—
An act of pure love
That encased all the power that we cannot fathom into
Skin that breaks and tears and bleeds
This skin formed within a womb
That grew and stretched and bent until it
Released the King of the Universe
In blood and salty tears …
Some His own
Wonderful indeed

Counselor
The best advice in Heaven and on Earth
The most comforting shoulder to lean on
A defender on your behalf
Wisdom, constantly accessible
There is no need to navigate daily decisions
Big or small, on our own
The Counselor dwells within us
We merely ask, seek, knock
And He's there, ready with a response
And His response is
Full of wonder

Wonderful Counselor
Counsel full of wonder
No scholar am I, to draw a definitive line
But like a child I can sit in awe
Of the mystery that is Christ within me
I can express my gratitude for access to the mind of Christ
His thoughts that guide and
Provide a way forward for me, His beloved child
My ears hear the song announcing the One who dwells in me
Wonderful
Counselor

Prophecy

For to us a child is born, to us a son is given, and the government will be on his shoulders. And he will be called Wonderful Counselor, Mighty God, Everlasting Father, Prince of Peace.
Isaiah 9:6

Fulfillment

In order that they may know the mystery of God, namely, Christ, in whom are hidden all the treasures of wisdom and knowledge.
Colossians 2:2b–3

The gospels of Matthew, Mark, Luke, and John each illustrate the many ways Jesus is wonderful through His ability to teach, heal, set people free, and bring about the Kingdom of Heaven here on Earth.

Prayer

Jesus, you are wonderful. There are not enough words to describe how wonderful you truly are. Thank you for being my counselor, for allowing me access to your mind (1 Corinthians 2:16b), for guiding me, and filling me with your wisdom. Amen.

Going Deeper

Consider worshiping by listening to Handel's *Messiah* today and letting the words about who Christ is sink deep within your heart.

If you have a problem, conflict, or challenge you're facing, invite Jesus into it, asking Him for counsel as to how to navigate or resolve the issue.

Christmas is a season full of wonder, and children experience wonder so beautifully. Look for ways to be childlike today, experience this glorious season as if it were the first time.

Additional Study

Romans 14:11; Philippians 2:5–11; 1 Corinthians 2:16b; John 14:26 (CSB); Matthew 7:7–8; Colossians 1:27

REFLECTIONS

DECEMBER 16

For to us a child is born, to us a son is given, and the government will be on his shoulders. And he will be called Wonderful Counselor, Mighty God, Everlasting Father, Prince of Peace.
Isaiah 9:6

Mighty God

I think it's fairly safe to say we all want a mighty God
If I can do what a god can then what do I need one for?
But there's so much going on behind the scenes with this name
You see the Israelites wanted a Savior
Who would literally smite the Romans and
Save them as a people group from tyrannical reign
An almighty god who came in power and
Showed off his strength and
Called down fire and hail like in the days of their forefathers
But that wasn't what Jesus was coming for
His savior mission was for captive souls, not captive bodies

This name of Jesus establishes His fullness of divinity
For He holds all power and authority
It's almost as if Isaiah was paving the way
For the Israelites to comprehend
That a man would be the vessel but
He would be more than they could see

Did Mary reflect on these words as she snuggled her son?
How Yahweh could send the fullness of Himself
In mere pounds and ounces
Did she wonder if He'd be the warrior savior?
Or did she know in the depths of her heart
That all that divinity was racing through the DNA of a babe
Who would sacrifice His life for a world He loved?

All we can do is ponder
Wonder
Study the Hebrew, the Greek, the Aramaic for clues
But the wonder of it all is that Jesus knew
At least, I think He did, even that may be debatable
But let's imagine together
A baby, a toddler potty training
A child who skins his knees and plays and laughs and cries
A teenager learning the craft of his father
And a young man mourning the loss of his lifelong teacher
A man, by obedience and not requirement,
Pushed under water and brought to the surface
Hearing the audible voice of home declaring His love
And the awareness that He lived enveloped in fragility
Yet His birthright was a level of power and authority
We can't wrap our minds around this side of eternity

It took a Mighty God to lay down His life
It took a Mighty God to resurrect into new life
And this Mighty God
Is the same baby we celebrate each Christmas
Power and authority
Nestled in a manger
For all the world to see

Prophecy

For to us a child is born, to us a son is given, and the government will be on his shoulders. And he will be called Wonderful Counselor, Mighty God, Everlasting Father, Prince of Peace.
Isaiah 9:6

Fulfillment

Just as the Son of Man did not come to be served, but to serve, and to give his life as a ransom for many.
Matthew 20:28

Who, being in very nature God, did not consider equality with God something to be used to his own advantage; rather, he made himself nothing by taking the very nature of a servant, being made in human likeness. And being found in appearance as a man, he humbled himself by becoming obedient to death—even death on a cross! Therefore God exalted him to the highest place and gave him the name that is above every name, that at the name of Jesus every knee should bow, in heaven and on earth and under the earth, and every tongue acknowledge that Jesus Christ is Lord, to the glory of God the Father.
Philippians 2:6–11

Prayer

Jesus, you are Mighty God. I am in awe that you, as God, would become like me, a human, in order to provide a way for me to be reconciled to you and the Father. Thank you for the sacrifice you made in coming as a human and laying your glorious life down as a ransom for me. Amen.

Going Deeper

When you hear the name "Mighty God," what comes to mind?

How does the frailty of Jesus coming as a human infant stretch the way you think about Him as Mighty God?

Additional Study

Luke 19:10; Matthew 3:13–17

REFLECTIONS

DECEMBER 17

For to us a child is born, to us a son is given, and the government will be on his shoulders. And he will be called Wonderful Counselor, Mighty God, Everlasting Father, Prince of Peace.
Isaiah 9:6

Everlasting Father

Everyone has a different relationship with the word father
It's complicated and complex for some
And a beloved endearment for others
God as Father can induce fear in some
And loving devotion in others
Whatever your relationship with the concept of Father
God is better than anything you've experienced
And could possibly imagine

The ancient text we hold as Truth
Describes God as Father, Jesus as Son
And Holy Spirit as three in one
Yet Isaiah describes the Messiah as
Everlasting Father
Which presents a bit of a conundrum
Can the Son be the Father?
Are they both/and?
These verses won't attempt a theological dissection
Rather, an exploration into mystery seems to be
The path of discovery

A father protects his children
Jesus calls Himself the Door of the sheep
Keeping watch over us and protecting us

A father provides for his family
Jesus calls Himself the Bread of Life
He sustains us with such a feast we will never know hunger

A father gives his children their identity
Jesus calls Himself the True Vine
We are the branches that grow from His vine
The more we abide in Him
The more He reveals who He is within us

A father provides guidance for his children
Jesus is the Light of the World
Illuminating the way for us to follow
For He is also the Way, the Truth, and the Life

A father makes sacrifices for those entrusted to him
Jesus is the Good Shepherd
Who lays down His life for His sheep
He is the Resurrection and the Life
Who not only laid His life down, but was raised into new life
Which He promised to us, His dearly loved children

It's a mystery to me how the Son can be the Father
But it is a mystery I embrace with childlike faith
Jesus fulfills the role of a father to perfection
Never having had a natural child
He simply saw what His Father was doing and
Followed His perfect example
And we, His children, will bask in His love as our
Everlasting Father throughout eternity

Prophecy

For to us a child is born, to us a son is given, and the government will be on his shoulders. And he will be called Wonderful Counselor, Mighty God, Everlasting Father, Prince of Peace.
Isaiah 9:6

Fulfillment

I and the Father are one … the Father is in me, and I in the Father.
John 10:30, 38b

Prayer

Jesus, my Everlasting Father, you are the perfect revelation of God the Father. Thank you for revealing who God is through your life on this earth. It's exciting to think about how you are revealing the character of God throughout eternity! I can be connected to God today because of who you are and all that you have done for me. Help me to continue to learn about all the ways that you are showing me who God is. Amen.

Going Deeper

Pick a few of Jesus's "I Am" statements and read the verses associated with them. Dialogue with God about how Jesus is revealing His character and nature as Father through those verses. (I am the Door: John 10:9; I am the Bread of Life: John 6:35; I am the Vine: John 15:1, 5; I am the Light of the World: John 8:12; I am the Way and the Truth and the Life: John 14:6; I am the Good Shepherd: John 10:11, 14; I am the Resurrection and the Life: John 11:25.)

Take a few moments to connect with Jesus. Ask Him to bring you deeper revelation on how He is the Everlasting Father. (For further reflection, read Colossians 1:15–23 through the lens of Jesus as the Everlasting Father.)

Additional Study

John 5:19; 6:35; 8:12; 10:9; 11; 14; 11:25; 14:6; 9; 15:1

REFLECTIONS

DECEMBER 18

For to us a child is born, to us a son is given, and the government will be on his shoulders. And he will be called Wonderful Counselor, Mighty God, Everlasting Father, Prince of Peace.
Isaiah 9:6

Prince of Peace

Shalom
Perfection found its fullness in
The Creator of Heaven and Earth
Complete was an open loop
Until closure was found in Yahweh
Wholeness is the being of God Himself
Shalom
Peace that means so much more than peace

The Ancient of Days' perfect vision for mankind, distorted
His creation, wayward
Wholeness, fractured
Completeness, fragmented
Perfection, blemished
Restoration needed

A Son who could represent His Father
A Prince carrying
The proclamation of healing for the fractures
Restoration of the fragmented
Blemishes wiped clean
Shalom

A Prince delivering peace
Peace that unifies
Peace that heals
Peace that restores
Peace that guards hearts and minds
Peace that keeps
Shalom peace that brings wholeness, completion, perfection

How fitting that the Prince of Peace
Arrived in the midst of a census
Organized by an occupying army
Wholeness grew within a virgin
Whose relationships were fractured
Completion took His first breath in
A fragmented country
Perfection Himself arrived imperfectly
Born in blood and water
Shalom

The Kingdom is made of
Righteousness, peace, and joy
Jesus, the Son of the King
The One whose righteousness made you and I new
The One who was anointed with the oil of exceeding joy
The One who administers shalom
Jesus, our Prince of Peace

Prophecy

For to us a child is born, to us a son is given, and the government will be on his shoulders. And he will be called Wonderful Counselor, Mighty God, Everlasting Father, Prince of Peace.
Isaiah 9:6

Fulfillment

Peace I leave with you; my peace I give you. I do not give to you as the world gives. Do not let your hearts be troubled and do not be afraid.
John 14:27

For he himself is our peace, who has made the two groups one and has destroyed the barrier, the dividing wall of hostility, by setting aside in his flesh the law with its commands and regulations. His purpose was to create in himself one new humanity out of the two, thus making peace, and in one body to reconcile both of them to God through the cross, by which he put to death their hostility. He came and preached peace to you who were far away and peace to those who were near.
Ephesians 2:14–17

Prayer

Prince of Peace, thank you for continual access to perfect peace, to shalom. I invite you into every area of my life that needs your peace. I lay down my anxious thoughts and welcome the shalom of God into each one, for you alone can bring true peace no matter the circumstances. Thank you for guarding my heart and mind with your peace (Philippians 4:7). Amen.

Going Deeper

Read John 14:27 in the Fulfillment section. What do you think Jesus meant when He said, "I do not give to you as the world gives?"

Ask the Lord to bring to mind a time when you experienced His perfect peace. Journal how that felt. In the midst of this busy season, ask Jesus to increase your experience of His peace in your life. When challenges arise, turn Philippians 4:6–7 into a prayer: "Do not be anxious about anything, but in every situation, by prayer and petition, with thanksgiving, present your requests to God. And the peace of God, which transcends all understanding, will guard your hearts and your minds in Christ Jesus."

Additional Study

Genesis 3; Luke 4:14–21; Philippians 4:7; Luke 2:1–7; Romans 14:17; Hebrews 1:9

REFLECTIONS

DECEMBER 19

Of the greatness of his government and peace there will be no end. He will reign on David's throne and over his kingdom, establishing and upholding it with justice and righteousness from that time on and forever. The zeal of the Lord Almighty will accomplish this.
Isaiah 9:7

A Never-ending Kingdom

Egyptian chains shackled hands and feet
Gaunt Hebrew men bent down in defeat
Pharaoh
Frightened by the sea of foreign humanity
Increased the load
Decreasing their hope
Releasing a desperate cry
Deliver us

Giants in the land
Struck fear in the hearts of all but two men
Millions of wanderers wondering
Where all that wandering was leading
Yet refusing to enter the Promised Land
Only Joshua and Caleb took a stand
But rebellion sealed the Hebrews' fate
Into the wilderness, forty years to wait

The Promised Land finally attained
But relationship with Yahweh was under strain
From Moses to Joshua, and judge to king
Prophets a message of hope did bring
Each breath spent releasing the decree
That a Messiah was coming for you and for me
Hope was not lost, but instead could be found
In a future prophet and priest and king to be crowned

Oh but how misguided so many were
Looking for rescue in a warrior, a disrupter
But the Messiah came instead as a babe
Crying and helpless and as He was raised
He embraced His assignment as the King to be
But He did so first on bended knee
Modeling service, humility, and love
Reflecting the image of His Father above

Son of David and Son of Man
Christ the fulfillment of God's redemption plan
The everlasting King from David's line
King of Heaven and Earth now for all time
Gabriel promised His mother Mary
That His Kingdom would know no end you see
Just as Isaiah declared and decreed
There will be no end of His government or peace

Prophecy

Of the greatness of his government and peace there will be no end. He will reign on David's throne and over his kingdom, establishing and upholding it with justice and righteousness from that time on and forever. The zeal of the Lord Almighty will accomplish this.
Isaiah 9:7

Fulfillment

The Son is the image of the invisible God, the firstborn over all creation. For in him all things were created: things in heaven and on earth, visible and invisible, whether thrones or powers or rulers or authorities; all things have been created through him and for him. He is before all things, and in him all things hold together. And he is the head of the body, the church; he is the beginning and the firstborn from among the dead, so that in everything he might have the supremacy.
Colossians 1:15–18

Prayer

Jesus, thank you that I can rest in you, knowing that your government and peace will know no end. Your Kingdom is secure and I have a place there! You created all things and are holding them together. You reign supreme. It is incredible to be a co-heir with you, Jesus, and a citizen of your eternal Kingdom. Amen.

Going Deeper

How does knowing that Jesus is supreme above all earthly governments make you feel? What do you see as your role as a citizen of the Kingdom of Heaven?

Today's devotion touches on a few of Israel's challenges when it came to governmental authority and peace. Read through the story of the Israelites being freed from Egypt and dialogue with God about how He showed up for His people during this time. Ask Him how He wants to show up for you today in your life. (Exodus 1–14)

Additional Study

Exodus 1; Numbers 13:26–33; Luke 1:26–38

REFLECTIONS

DECEMBER 20

*A shoot will come up from the stump of Jesse; from his
roots a Branch will bear fruit.*
Isaiah 11:1

A New Branch

David the shepherd, the boy who would be king
The defeater of giants
The one of whom the people sing
David the musician, the worshiper, the friend
The warrior, the leader, the inquirer
The one who drew together the mightiest of men

Oh to have been David in that day and age
To have walked and talked with God and been
The one on whom Holy Spirit stayed
A prophet who penned words fulfilled
A priest who worshiped as if the veil were already torn
A king who battled for victory
Until every enemy was overcome

Precious son of Jesse
A man after God's own heart
He revealed a glimpse of Heaven's plan
His life on this earth marked
The archetype of the Anointed One
What it might look like when time grew full
And birthed God's own Son

Out of the stump of Jesse will grow a shoot
The Son of David
A new branch bearing fruit from the old root
Hope out of devastation
Ages of waiting kissed the moment of promise
And with that kiss came great celebration

Oh to have seen Jesus in those days
To have walked with Him and talked with Him
And been one with whom He laughed and played
A prophet like Moses
Closing the gap between God and man
A priest offering the ultimate sacrifice
A king before the world began

Jesus, the new branch, Son of David, Son of Man
Son of God, the carpenter, the builder
The rabbi, the lamb
The gatherer of disciples
The boy lost for a few days
The babe, the promised one
The Word made flesh
Flesh that would pay

The root of Jesse bore Jesus
Open our eyes that we may see
The power and possibility of legacy

Prophecy

A shoot will come up from the stump of Jesse; from his roots a Branch will bear fruit.
Isaiah 11:1

Fulfillment

For I tell you that Christ has become a servant of the Jews on behalf of God's truth, so that the promises made to the patriarchs might be confirmed and, moreover, that the Gentiles might glorify God for his mercy.... And again, Isaiah says, "The Root of Jesse will spring up, one who will arise to rule over the nations; in him the Gentiles will hope."
Romans 15:8–9a, 12

Prayer

Jesus, reveal to me the possibilities of what could be with my legacy. How can I leave behind a personal legacy, and how can I pray for those who will come after me in my family line? May everyone in my family come to know you, Jesus, the Branch from the root of Jesse, the true Messiah!
Amen.

Going Deeper

1 Samuel 16:7b says, "The Lord does not look at the things people look at. People look at the outward appearance, but the Lord looks at the heart." The context for this verse is when the prophet Samuel was examining Jesse's sons to hear from the Lord on which would be king. It wasn't the oldest, strongest, most handsome son who was chosen, but the youngest, David, who was out tending to the animals. David became the greatest king Israel would have. Do you find comfort in the fact that the Lord looks at the heart rather than appearance? What does this verse tell us about what is important to God?

Take some time to journal what you want to be remembered for. Journal about what you want to leave as your legacy. Ask God to examine your heart, and begin a work in you that will outlive you, blessing others.

Additional Study

1 Samuel 16–17; 2 Samuel 6; Galatians 4:4; Deuteronomy 18:15; John 1:1–14

REFLECTIONS

DECEMBER 21

In that day the Root of Jesse will stand as a banner for the peoples; the nations will rally to him, and his resting place will be glorious.
Isaiah 11:10

Banner of Salvation

Imagine being a shepherd
Getting a little dirtier than your neighbor perhaps
As you do a necessary job
In the heat of day and cold of night
Keeping hundreds of not so bright, smelly sheep
In some kind of order so they eat, and drink, and grow
Not to mention protecting them from wild animals, thieves
And their own ineptness

Can you imagine settling in for the night
Finishing off your last sip of water
As you say goodnight to your fellow herders
Making your way to your pallet under the stars
Another day gone, another night of rest ahead
That may or may not be peaceful
The gentle baa's of your charges echoing as they too settle in
Huddling close for warmth

Abruptly
The layers of the night sky peel back and
The most magnificent being appears
He decrees:
Fear not! I bring good news of great joy!
Today, in the town of David the Savior has been born!
He is the Messiah
And you will find him wrapped in cloths lying in a manger

Stunned, you don't know what to do or say
Could it be true? And if so, why are they telling you?!
A shepherd, getting ready for bed!

Suddenly a host of heavenly beings appears—
Are they angels?
These apparitions begin to release a sound so captivating
You can only stop and stare
Wondering if they are really there
But they must be, your fellow shepherds are immobile,
Staring into the sky as well
And suddenly the song rings out clearly
And you realize this is not a dream
It's actually happening
Glory to God in the highest, they sing
And on earth, peace on whom His favor rests!
Who does that include, you wonder

Moments later you come to your senses and
Race to the manger as if drawn by a beacon
And there He is, just as they said
Wrapped up in cloths
Nestled in his mother's chest
The Messiah, the Anointed One
The Hope of Israel has come!

As you behold this wondrous sight,
Lessons from your rabbi come to mind
Those cloths, the swaddling cloths
Wrapped round and round, tucking
The Christ child into comfort
Remind you of Isaiah's words:
The Root of Jesse will stand as a banner for the peoples

As days and years go by you wonder if
As Mary and Joseph wrapped and unwrapped
This promised child
Did they see Him in their mind's eye
Lifted up, people rallying to Him?
Did Isaiah's words ring in the back of their minds
As they do yours?
His resting place will be glorious
What did they think that meant?
You think of David's psalm which speaks of
Green pastures and quiet waters
Surely that's the kind of resting place Isaiah meant
Or could it mean more?

Many shepherds have come and gone
Since the angel's divine pronouncement
Yet Isaiah's prophetic utterance
Continues to rally the nations
Pointing us to the Banner of our Salvation
The babe in the manger wrapped up in swaddling cloth
The lamb on the beam with arms stretched wide
Inviting all who will look upon His face to enter in
To His glorious resting place

Prophecy

In that day the Root of Jesse will stand as a banner for the peoples; the nations will rally to him, and his resting place will be glorious.
Isaiah 11:10

Fulfillment

I, Jesus, have sent my angel to give you this testimony for the churches. I am the Root and the Offspring of David, and the bright Morning Star.
Revelation 22:16

Prayer

You, Jesus, are the Banner of Salvation that has been longed for throughout the ages. Thank you for coming not to condemn the world, but to save it. I rest in the finished work of the cross, grateful for your resurrection and life, all made possible through your coming as a baby to take my place. Amen.

Going Deeper:

While we have no way of knowing, this side of Heaven, what the shepherds were thinking as they experienced that special night, it's interesting to explore what thoughts may have raced through their minds. Of the prophecies you've read about thus far, which holds the most wonder for you? Thank God for speaking through His prophets about the salvation He promised.

Read Isaiah 11:1–10.
This passage gives us a beautiful glimpse into eternity. Spend time today thanking God for the fulfillment of these promises through the gift of Jesus.

Additional Study

Luke 2:1–21; Psalm 23

REFLECTIONS

DECEMBER 22

See, I will send the prophet Elijah to you before that great and dreadful day of the Lord comes. He will turn the hearts of the parents to their children, and the hearts of the children to their parents; or else I will come and strike the land with total destruction.
Malachi 4:5–6

The Forerunner

Four hundred years of silence
Followed Malachi's prophecies
Did Israel wonder where Yahweh was
And why no prophet came forth

Did they cling to the Torah
Or was it memorized by rote
Were Isaiah's writings read
And studied and pored over
Or did they just … wait

With each Passover and festival
Did they maintain hope
Or did they exhale familiar sayings
Without faith

And after 400 years
What went through their minds when
The silence was broken by
An eccentric man who lived in the wilderness
But came to town preaching repentance

Prepare the way of the Lord
Salvation is coming
Prepare the way of the Lord

Malachi prophesied
The prophet Elijah would come
Turning the hearts of the fathers to their sons
And the sons to their fathers
And what is the turning of a heart but repentance
To turn around

Isaiah prophesied a voice in the wilderness
And John the Baptist himself said
I am the voice of one calling out in the wilderness
Make straight the way for the Lord

Before salvation arrived
He was heralded
Like a king announced
God sent the Baptizer
The voice preaching repentance and restoration
And salvation to come
The last of the prophets of old
Carried these words as a baton
Toward the finish line of the last sacrifice

The One whose sandals I am unworthy to remove is coming
The One who has been prophesied has come
And will baptize in water and fire
He must be greater, I must be less

This prophet, who even in the womb
Leapt at the proximity of the seed of the Savior
Eliciting a proclamation from his own mother
That the Christ was near
This prophet prepared the way for the promised one
Crying
Prepare the way of the Lord for
Salvation is here

Prophecy

See, I will send the prophet Elijah to you before that great and dreadful day of the Lord comes. He will turn the hearts of the parents to their children, and the hearts of the children to their parents; or else I will come and strike the land with total destruction.
Malachi 4:5–6

A voice of one calling: "In the wilderness prepare the way for the Lord; make straight in the desert a highway for our God. Every valley shall be raised up, every mountain and hill made low; the rough ground shall become level, the rugged places a plain."
Isaiah 40:3–4

Fulfillment

For he will be great in the sight of the Lord. He is never to take wine or other fermented drink, and he will be filled with the Holy Spirit even before he is born. He will bring back many of the people of Israel to the Lord their God.
Luke 1:15–16

John replied in the words of Isaiah the prophet, "I am the voice of one calling in the wilderness, 'Make straight the way for the Lord.'"
John 1:23

Prayer

Father, thank you for speaking through the prophets of what was to come. Thank you for the gift of John the Baptist, who, like Elijah, returned hearts back to you. If there is anything in my heart that I need to repent for, I lay that before you today, turning away from sin and embracing your love and forgiveness. Amen.

Going Deeper

Just as God promised literal signs of the coming of Christ (Days 10–13), He also promised a forerunner, someone who would come before Jesus and prepare the way for His ministry. Why do you think this forerunner was necessary?

Jesus Himself tells us that John was the final prophet of the old covenant (Luke 16:16). Read Luke 3:1–20. In what ways does John foreshadow Jesus's life and ministry?

Additional Study

John 1:19–34; John 3:30; Luke 16:16; Luke 1:41

REFLECTIONS

DECEMBER 23

In the sixth month of Elizabeth's pregnancy, God sent the angel Gabriel to Nazareth, a town in Galilee, to a virgin pledged to be married to a man named Joseph, a descendant of David. The virgin's name was Mary. The angel went to her and said, "Greetings, you who are highly favored! The Lord is with you." Mary was greatly troubled at his words and wondered what kind of greeting this might be. But the angel said to her, "Do not be afraid, Mary; you have found favor with God. You will conceive and give birth to a son, and you are to call him Jesus. He will be great and will be called the Son of the Most High. The Lord God will give him the throne of his father David, and he will reign over Jacob's descendants forever; his kingdom will never end."
Luke 1:26–33

The Annunciation

Only God would trust the salvation of the world
To a fourteen-year-old girl
We're familiar with the story so
We may not always stop to ask questions
But allow me to pose one:
What would you trust to a fourteen-year-old?

These days most can't even date until at least sixteen
Nor can they drive, or live alone
In fact it will be eleven more years until
Their prefrontal cortex is developed enough to
Weigh consequences and make decisions
With a fully developed brain

And God, the Creator, who designed our brains
To not fully develop until the age of twenty-five
Chose a fourteen-year-old to carry the
Word made flesh
And if He chose her for that—
What might He be entrusting to you?

But I digress ... there's more to explore

Not only did God make this unusual choice
But He also sent an archangel, Gabriel,
To deliver this message
Considering we only know of three archangels
In the ancient, inspired text of our faith
Can you imagine what he may have looked like when he appeared?
Scripture seems to indicate that angelic appearances
Were more normal than they are today
Now that's something to think about, is it not?
And every time they appear their first words are
Do not fear
Which immediately suggests
Their first impression strikes fear
But unlike many men before her
Mary didn't fall down as though dead
That's my girl
She was too busy thinking about what it meant
That she had found favor with the Lord

What accomplishments do you think she had to her name?
She was betrothed, yet unwed, and in this time
Women were considered property
There was no amount of productivity
That would gain her any sense of notoriety
All she really could do was just ... be

And in her being—
God found something He could work with
Now that's a whole word right there

Instead of falling down Mary waited patiently
Silently pondering, wondering
What this supernatural being was bringing

Gabriel continued ... *you will conceive and give birth*
Whoa whoa whoa, let's pause right there
Now he said more after that, but this is where I think
Mary stopped listening for a second
Because after all of Gabriel's decree she said
How can this be for I am not married

She knew about the birds and the bees
And that there's no way this could come to pass
Without another participant in the mix

Then Gabriel dropped the clincher that cinched it all up
The Holy Spirit will come upon you
And the Lord will provide the seed

In my mind, this is where Mary may have gone weak-kneed

Did she know the prophecies?
Women weren't taught by the rabbis—
Did she know Isaiah's words about a virgin conceiving?
Was this all new information or was there a moment of realization?
This is all speculation—
The text we have makes no mention of her physical reaction
But may I remind you once again she was likely fourteen
Fourteen then and fourteen now surely have some differences
But it's hard to wrap the mind around the weight
That God was entrusting to her shoulders

Gabriel laid it out, clear as day—the throne of David would be His
And all of Jacob's descendants would be blessed and
His government would never end
Surely these prophecies were well rehearsed and reinforced and
Realization began to forge into faith and acceptance

Let it be unto me as you have said

Surrender
Acceptance of all that was to come her way
The whispers, the ridicule, the judgment
The risk of her entire future
At fourteen she weighed the cost and laid down her life
In exchange for God's plan

Which was that His Son
Her son
Would lay down His life for her

And for you

But first

He would enter this world as one of us
Laying down access to His God-nature
And becoming a child of a fourteen-year-old mom
Whom God chose to birth the Light of the World

Prophecy

In the sixth month of Elizabeth's pregnancy, God sent the angel Gabriel to Nazareth, a town in Galilee, to a virgin pledged to be married to a man named Joseph, a descendant of David. The virgin's name was Mary. The angel went to her and said, "Greetings, you who are highly favored! The Lord is with you." Mary was greatly troubled at his words and wondered what kind of greeting this might be. But the angel said to her, "Do not be afraid, Mary; you have found favor with God. You will conceive and give birth to a son, and you are to call him Jesus. He will be great and will be called the Son of the Most High. The Lord God will give him the throne of his father David, and he will reign over Jacob's descendants forever; his kingdom will never end."
Luke 1:26–33

Fulfillment

This is how the birth of Jesus the Messiah came about: His mother Mary was pledged to be married to Joseph, but before they came together, she was found to be pregnant through the Holy Spirit … an angel of the Lord appeared to him in a dream and said, "Joseph son of David, do not be afraid to take Mary home as your wife, because what is conceived in her is from the Holy Spirit. She will give birth to a son, and you are to give him the name Jesus, because he will save his people from their sins." … When Joseph woke up, he did what the angel of the Lord had commanded him and took Mary home as his wife. But he did not consummate their marriage until she gave birth to a son. And he gave him the name Jesus.
Matthew 1:18, 20–21, 24–25

Prayer

Father, thank you for the example of Mary. Help me to be as obedient to you as she was, and to surrender quickly. Increase my faith for the assignments you entrust me with. Amen.

Going Deeper

It's easy to become so familiar with this story that we miss the nuance and wonder of these moments. Read Luke 1–2 and Matthew 1, asking God to give you fresh eyes for this story. Put yourself in Mary's shoes, and in Joseph's. Think about the risk they took in saying yes to this call, and how they would have been treated. What did choosing to carry Jesus do to Mary's reputation? Why do you think she so quickly surrendered to the Lord's call on her life?

Were you surprised by Mary's age? How does it make you feel that God chose someone so young to carry out such a world-altering task? How will this knowledge affect how you look at young people?

Additional Study

Luke 1:26–38; Philippians 2:5–8; John 8:12

REFLECTIONS

DECEMBER 24

At that time Mary got ready and hurried to a town in the hill country of Judea, where she entered Zechariah's home and greeted Elizabeth. When Elizabeth heard Mary's greeting, the baby leaped in her womb, and Elizabeth was filled with the Holy Spirit. In a loud voice she exclaimed: "Blessed are you among women, and blessed is the child you will bear! But why am I so favored, that the mother of my Lord should come to me? As soon as the sound of your greeting reached my ears, the baby in my womb leaped for joy. Blessed is she who has believed that the Lord would fulfill his promises to her!"
Luke 1:39–45

Two Women

While the exchange between Elizabeth and Mary
Recorded in Luke is not technically prophecy
Regarding Christ's birth
I ask your grace in using this space to explore
The beauty of this moment and what it speaks to

Two women
One old and beyond childbearing years
The other young, never having known a man
One trusting in the faithfulness of her God despite the odds
The other favored, yet, until recently
Unaware of just how much
Both blessed with unusual blessings

An old woman, now with child
Visualize the wrinkles near her eyes
As she smiles while resting brown-spotted hands upon
The expanding belly that shocked her village

A young girl, now with child
Visualize the wonder and apprehension in her eyes
As she steels herself to tell her betrothed
And prays he doesn't leave her an outcast in her village

Mary, desperate to share this journey
With someone who could understand
Seeks out Elizabeth
Two women with miracle babies in the womb
As Mary approaches,
Holy Spirit falls upon Elizabeth
Who proclaims Mary as the mother of her Lord!
The Christ is revealed first to two women
Even in utero Jesus's mission began
Demonstrating the equality between woman and man
Elevating women beyond property and into personhood
It was just the beginning of all that He would shake up!

Furthermore, Mary bursts into praise
Prophesying that she will be called blessed for all days
She celebrates the mercy of God
His faithfulness to His people
His remembrance of the covenant He has made

As we ponder this passage we must consider
When faced with unusual, though welcome
Answers to prayer
In spite of fear, or worry
Can we respond with faith and praise
And do so in community with others who will also believe?

As this precious eve is upon us
Will you revel in the wonder of
The disruptions to the status quo this Babe brought about
The praise He inspires, despite fear and doubt
The faith He invites us into, even so far as
Believing for impossibility
His conception alone reveals that impossible is
One of His specialties

Blessed among women is Mary
Her faith became sight
And Elizabeth reveals God's timing is right
Two women, plucked out of obscurity and
Remembered for all eternity

Scripture

At that time Mary got ready and hurried to a town in the hill country of Judea, where she entered Zechariah's home and greeted Elizabeth. When Elizabeth heard Mary's greeting, the baby leaped in her womb, and Elizabeth was filled with the Holy Spirit. In a loud voice she exclaimed: "Blessed are you among women, and blessed is the child you will bear! But why am I so favored, that the mother of my Lord should come to me? As soon as the sound of your greeting reached my ears, the baby in my womb leaped for joy. Blessed is she who has believed that the Lord would fulfill his promises to her!"
Luke 1:39–45

Prayer

Father, thank You that you are a promise keeper. Thank you for always being on time. Thank you for erasing all lines of hierarchy among your children (Galatians 3:28). Thank you, Jesus, for disrupting the status quo and revealing the heart and character of God to mankind. Amen.

Going Deeper

Read Luke 1:1–56 to further study Elizabeth and Mary's story. While Mary's pregnancy surely created talk in the town, Elizabeth's must've been viewed as a miracle. Mary's pregnancy was arguably the greatest miracle in history.

Do you need a miracle right now? As we celebrate the eve of our Savior's birth, bring your need before our miracle-working God.

In addition to elevating and valuing women, what other disruptions did Jesus bring about during His life? What can we learn about who God is from these disruptions to the status quo of the day?

Additional Study

Galatians 3:28–29

REFLECTIONS

DECEMBER 25

His father Zechariah was filled with the Holy Spirit and prophesied: "Praise be to the Lord, the God of Israel, because he has come to his people and redeemed them. He has raised up a horn of salvation for us in the house of his servant David (as he said through his holy prophets of long ago), salvation from our enemies and from the hand of all who hate us—to show mercy to our ancestors and to remember his holy covenant, the oath he swore to our father Abraham: to rescue us from the hand of our enemies, and to enable us to serve him without fear in holiness and righteousness before him all our days."
Luke 1:67–75

A Rescuer Has Come

Zechariah, faithful priest, husband
Elizabeth, of the line of Aaron, wife
A couple who served the Lord
Yet longed for more

A child to complete their family tree
Bringing their number from two to three
Yet the window of fertility closed with age
Covered with the curtain of shame
Back then, barrenness—a sign of the displeasure of God
People must have wondered
If perhaps some sin prevented this desire

As Zechariah served his duties at Temple
An encounter in the Holy of Holies
With the messenger Gabriel changed everything
Prayers answered, a child would be given
In shock, Zechariah expressed disbelief
Too old are we, how can this be

For his questioning
The angel rendered him mute until the birth of his child
Let this a lesson to us be
Faith in the Creator of miracles is required

Nine months later, a child in his arms
Zechariah's tongue was loosened
And he prophesied:
As the holy prophets of old have declared
He has raised a horn of salvation for us
From the house of David
And in fulfillment of His oath to Abraham
A rescuer has come
Redemption is at hand

This rescuer was then six months in the womb
Years away from stepping into
The fullness of His time
Yet ...
The birth that we celebrate this day
This Lamb of God, our Redeemer, our Rescuer
Is one that has been prophesied over
Thousands of years
Through faithful messengers
Assuring His people of the deliverance to come

The moment of the Messiah's birth
When head and shoulders and body burst forth
Words of prophecy met their fulfillment
Only a God outside of space and time
Could weave together such a perfect rhyme
In text after text, the proof you can see
But faith is required for the depth of this mystery
For God so loved you and me
He sent His Son to become like us
Salvation is coming, the prophets of old cried out
With the first cry of breath in human lungs
Jesus Himself announced
Salvation is here

Prophecy

His father Zechariah was filled with the Holy Spirit and prophesied: "Praise be to the Lord, the God of Israel, because he has come to his people and redeemed them. He has raised up a horn of salvation for us in the house of his servant David (as he said through his holy prophets of long ago), salvation from our enemies and from the hand of all who hate us—to show mercy to our ancestors and to remember his holy covenant, the oath he swore to our father Abraham: to rescue us from the hand of our enemies, and to enable us to serve him without fear in holiness and righteousness before him all our days."
Luke 1:67–75

Fulfillment

So Joseph also went up from the town of Nazareth in Galilee to Judea, to Bethlehem the town of David, because he belonged to the house and line of David. He went there to register with Mary, who was pledged to be married to him and was expecting a child. While they were there, the time came for the baby to be born, and she gave birth to her firstborn, a son. She wrapped him in cloths and placed him in a manger, because there was no guest room available for them.
Luke 2:4–7

Prayer

Jesus, I celebrate your coming! Thank you for becoming like me, coming to Earth as a baby in order to bring salvation. You have redeemed and rescued me and I will be forever grateful. May your name be honored and lifted high today and always. Amen.

Going Deeper

Read John 1:1–18. Though not a traditional Christmas text, these verses so succinctly lay out who Jesus is and why He came. Spend time on verses 5 and 14. Ask God to speak to you through these verses and journal what you hear.

Why do you think God used prophecy over so many hundreds of years to announce what He was going to do to save His beloved people and the Gentiles? What can we learn about God based upon these and other prophecies that have come to pass in Scripture?

Additional Study

Luke 1:5–45; John 3:16

REFLECTIONS

CONCLUSION

The Word became flesh and made his dwelling among us. We have seen his glory, the glory of the one and only Son, who came from the Father, full of grace and truth.
John 1:14

From Genesis to the Gospels, the Law and the Prophets are illustrating the need for a savior. The Law was too great a burden to carry. The prophets: messengers seeing something to come and attempting to describe God's plan in a way the people could grasp. Word after word they were attempting to illustrate what we now experience as the Word made flesh: Jesus Christ.

While the Christmas story is incredibly familiar to many of us, my hope is that after reading through this devotional, some of that familiarity has been replaced with the wonder of a new perspective, perhaps a detail or two not before considered in the context of the grand and beautiful birth of our Savior. May we, as followers of the Way of Christ, not become so familiar with the beautiful gift of the Word that we miss out on something new He is revealing to us, or lose the wonder found in the pages of our Bible.

"Unto us a child is born, unto us, a Son is given!" As this holiday season concludes, I pray that the fulfillment of these prophecies regarding Christ's coming remain in your heart. For God so loved you, that He sent His only Son on your behalf. God spoke of Jesus's coming through the ages, and He kept His word. We serve a God we can trust, a God who is good, a God whose love endures forever.

Merry Christmas!

ACKNOWLEDGMENTS

I would like to extend my deepest gratitude to the many who helped make this book possible. To my patient husband, Jake, thank you for supporting all of my retreats and giving me so much space to write. To Judy Brady, the best mother-in-love I could've asked for, thank you for taking care of me when I got such a bad cold while writing at your house! To Luis and Krystel Fortun, thank you for sharing your home with me as a writing get-away, and to Sandy Gledhill, thank you for hosting such an amazing writing retreat that challenged me in so many ways! To Tracy Erwin, who inspired me to keep wrestling with one of the prophecies until I found the words.

I'm grateful for the many resources available online, and this article provided by Jesusfilm.org was particularly helpful:

https://www.jesusfilm.org/blog/old-testament-prophecies/

Many thanks to my advance readers for your feedback: Hillary, Brittany, and Annie. Your comments were so incredibly helpful and allowed me to communicate concepts more deeply. Thank you to Kendra Duran for your brilliant copyediting skills, and to Sarah Wind for your eagle-eyed proofreading of the final manuscript!

To Jandré, thank you for bringing my dream cover to life! To Katie Hall, your advice has been invaluable and I'm so grateful for your wisdom and expertise. To Mom, Dad, John, and family, as well as Lindsey, and the many who have supported this dream and provided encouragement along the way, you have my deep gratitude.

Thank You!

ALSO AVAILABLE

Romantic comedies tend to have this timeline for love: a meetcute in spring or summer, followed by an argument or breakup in the rainy fall, all resolved by Christmas in time for a kiss under the mistletoe! However, in real life, I have found love knows no season ... and thankfully, seasons change. Sunny, carefree summers have been the backdrop for gut-wrenching breakups. Cold and barren winters have been made warm with snuggles. That first glance, hearing his laugh, the moment your heart knows time is standing still, the thrill when she reaches for your hand ... attraction, romance, love ... it happens when it happens.

Emory's debut book, *Seasons Change: A Poetry Collection* is a gathering of poems that encompass her time as a single woman. From first date butterflies to heartbreaking endings, hope for what's to come to modern-day psalms, Emory explores the seasons we all go through as we long for love.

Available on the following platforms:

AMAZON

AUDIBLE

ABOUT THE AUTHOR

Emory is a spoken word artist, author, and speaker who believes words are powerful tools with the potential to create worlds. When her parents realized her bevy of words also came with a flair for the dramatic, they put her in the local theatre straightaway and a grand love affair for story was born. This love for story led her along a creative path as well as a spiritual one, and she has explored the story of God's love, as well as how to share it, since she was a child.

Emory currently resides in Redding, CA with her husband Jake and their dog Max. She loves to explore the beautiful outdoors, spend time with her loved ones, and create.

For more information about Emory, to book her for an event, or to contact her, please visit her website. Also, enjoy Emory's spoken word poetry by visiting and subscribing to her YouTube channel.

YOUTUBE

WEBSITE